FORT LEE PUBLIC LIBRARY, NJ
3 9117 09078474 2

12/10

J636.9
RUS
W9-CKI-716

GOATS

Jane Russell

Grolier
an imprint of
SCHOLASTIC
www.scholastic.com/librarypublishing

Published 2009 by Grolier
An Imprint of Scholastic Library Publishing
Old Sherman Turnpike
Danbury, Connecticut 06816

© 2009 Grolier

All rights reserved. Except for use in a review, no part of this book may be reproduced, stored in a retrieval system, or transmitted in any form, or by any means, electronic or mechanical, including photocopying, recording, or otherwise, without prior permission of Grolier.

For The Brown Reference Group plc
Project Editor: Jolyon Goddard
Picture Researchers: Clare Newman, Sophie Mortimer
Designer: Sarah Williams
Managing Editor: Tim Harris

Volume ISBN-13: 978-0-7172-8042-1
Volume ISBN-10: 0-7172-8042-X

Library of Congress Cataloging-in-Publication Data

Nature's children. Set 5.
p. cm.
Includes index.
ISBN-13: 978-0-7172-8084-1
ISBN-10: 0-7172-8084-5 (set)
1. Animals--Encyclopedias, Juvenile. I. Grolier Educational (Firm)
QL49.N386 2009
590.3--dc22
2008014674

Printed and bound in China

PICTURE CREDITS

Front Cover: **Shutterstock**: Peter Hansen.

Back Cover: **Shutterstock**|: 5607594264, Mircea Bezergheanu, Vasily A. Ilyinsky, Shi Yali.

Alamy: Michael Juno 46, Christopher McGowan 14, Robert Slade 33, Ewan Stevenson 18; **Corbis**: Richard Hutchings 22; **FLPA**: Nigel Cattlin 38; **Photolibrary.com**: 37, David Marsden 13; **Photoshot**: David Woodfall 45; **Shutterstock**: Dan Briski 2–3, Paul Cowan 10, Ecliptic blue 30, Eric Isselee 4, 29, Petr Jilek 42, Sebastian Knight 5, Chee-Onn Leong 20, Stephen Meese 17, Ariusz Nawrocki 41, Orientaly 26–27, Regien Paassen 6; **Still Pictures**: J. Klein and M. Hubert 9, Mangeat/Andia.fr 34.

Contents

FACT FILE: Goats

Class	Mammals (Mammalia)
Order	Even-toed hoofed animals (Artiodactyla)
Family	Cattle, antelope, sheep, and goats (Bovidae)
Genus	Goats, ibexes, markhors, and turs (*Capra*)
Species	Domestic and wild goats (*Capra aegagrus*)
Subspecies	Domestic goat (*Capra aegagrus hircus*)
World distribution	Domestic goats are farmed worldwide; wild goats live naturally in Asia and Europe
Habitat	Goats can survive in most habitats, including grasslands, desert, scrub, and mountains
Distinctive physical characteristics	Hollow horns that grow up and back without twisting; many goats have a beard; most males have a very strong odor
Habits	Domestic and wild goats like to live in herds; males often prefer to live on their own
Diet	Most types of plants, especially grass, young shoots, and the leaves of shrubs and trees

Introduction

Goats were first **domesticated** about 10,000 years ago in the Zagros Mountains of Iran. People used them for their hair, skin, meat, and milk. Goat's milk is easier for the human body to **digest** than cow's milk. In fact, goat's milk is sometimes called "universal milk" because it can be used to bottle-feed many other baby animals. The hair of some goats is fine and soft and is woven into luxury clothing. Many people now keep goats as pets. The sons of Abraham Lincoln even kept pet goats inside the White House!

There are more than 600 million goats worldwide.

All breeds of goats are descended from wild goats, which are still found in southern Europe and western Asia.

Different Breeds

Female goats are usually called **nannies**, although they are sometimes also known as does (DOZE) or mishas (MI-SHAZ). Male goats are usually called **billies**, but are also referred to as bucks or rams. **Neutered** males are called wethers. Males are neutered to make them less aggressive. Baby goats are called **kids**.

All domestic goats are members of the same species. However, there are many different kinds, or **breeds**, of domestic goats. Each breed has its own unique characteristics, such as the amount of milk the nannies produce, the texture of the hair, or the color of the coat. Breeders—people who raise goats—usually **mate** a nanny with a billy from the same breed. But, sometimes, they will mate one breed with another to produce a crossbred kid. The breeder does that in the hope that the kids will have the best characteristics from each breed.

Shapes and Sizes

The different breeds of goats are broadly grouped into dairy, meat, and fiber goats. Dairy goats are bred for their milk. Fiber goats are raised for the quality of their coat. Meat goats are muscular breeds that are eaten in many parts of the world.

Another group is companion, or pet, goats. These include miniature breeds. Miniature goats grow to about 17 inches (43 cm) tall at the shoulders. That's just more than half the height of the tallest breeds, such as the Nubian, which can grow to 30 inches (75 cm) at the shoulders.

Other breeds are raised for the quality of their skin, which is used for making leather products. Some goats are even bred to work as pack animals, pulling small carts or carrying loads. These breeds are particularly strong and do not tire easily.

Goats have coats of many different colors, or combinations of colors, including white, brown, and ebony black.

The tough hoofed feet of these dairy nannies from Greece are well suited to climbing the rugged terrain.

Dairy Goats

All female goats produce milk once they give birth to a kid. The nannies of meat and fiber breeds produce only enough milk for their kids. But dairy goats produce a lot more milk—enough to feed their kids and still be milked twice a day. To keep milk production going, dairy nannies must have kids every year. Some dairy goat owners use milking machines to milk their goats, although hand milking is still the norm in most parts of the world.

In the United States, the most popular dairy breed is probably the Nubian. This breed's milk is creamy with a fresh taste. Miniature breeds, such as the Nigerian dwarf, are often used for milk production, too—especially if there is not much space for the goats. Their milk is sweet and high in fat.

Universal Milk

Goat's milk is more nutritious than cow's milk. It is also easier for the human body to digest. That is good for people who are sick or very old. Goat's milk is also good for people who become bloated or have bellyaches after drinking cow's milk. That's because goat's milk contains less of the sugar **lactose** than cow's milk. Lactose can cause stomach pain and other symptoms in many people.

Goat's milk can be fed to most orphaned baby mammals. For this reason, it is sometimes called "universal milk." Like cow's milk, goat's milk is usually heat-treated, or **pasteurized**, to kill any harmful **bacteria** that it might contain. It can then be turned into yogurt, cheese, and other dairy products. Goat's butter is white—not yellow like cow's butter. Cheese made from goat's milk is the most common cheese in many countries. In France, it is called chèvre (SHEV-RUH) after the French word for "goat." Feta cheese is another well-known cheese. It comes from Greece. Feta is made from a blend of goat's and sheep's milk.

It takes an experienced dairy goat owner about 5 minutes to milk a goat.

The coat of Cashmere goats keeps them warm in temperatures as low as -4°F (-20°C). Their wool is used to make pashmina shawls.

Fiber Goats

Most goats have a layer of long, straight, coarse hair on the outside of their coat. Underneath, there is a soft, woolly layer that keeps the body warm, especially in winter. Goats raised for their hair—or fiber goats—originated in the Himalayan mountains in Asia. The best-known fiber breeds are **Cashmere**, Pygora, and Angora goats.

The very fine and soft under layer of woolly hair that Cashmere and Pygora goats produce is called cashmere. Cashmere fibers only grow once each year, so only about 4 ounces (100 g) can be harvested from each goat in a year. To harvest wool, a goat owner combs it out of the goat's coat. The whole process takes about a week! For that reason cashmere fibers are very valuable.

Angora goats do not have any coarse outer hair. Rather, they have long silky hair called mohair all over their body. This fleece grows continuously and is cut off to harvest the wool. Each goat can produce more than 10 pounds (4.5 kg) of mohair each year. Like cashmere, mohair is used to make luxury woolen clothing.

Meat Goats

Some goats are raised just for their meat. Meat from goats is commonly eaten in Asia, southern Europe, and South America. These goats are particularly muscular, which means that they produce more meat. One of the most popular meat goats is the South African Boer, which came to the United States in the early 1990s. "Fainting goats" are another popular meat breed. Smaller farms sometimes raise miniature breeds, such as the African pygmy, for meat.

The strongest young male meat goats are not slaughtered. They are used for breeding, instead. These males are kept apart from the other goats. They are very **territorial** and produce a strong scent to mark their territory. The rest of the males are farmed for their meat. These males are usually neutered, which makes them less smelly, less aggressive, and easier to handle.

Pygmy goats
originate from
western Africa.

Wild goats are at risk of being attacked by predators, such as eagles, wolves, and large cats.

Goat Senses

Goats have sharp senses. Their eyesight is excellent. They can see clearly much farther into the distance than humans can. They have color vision, too, typical of animals that are active during the day. A goat's eyes are placed on the sides of the head. That gives the goat the ability to see almost all around itself. A goat's eyesight is well suited for spotting hunters, or predators.

A goat's hearing is especially sensitive to high-pitched sounds, such as the bleats of other goats. Their sense of smell is well developed. Like many other animals, goats have a **Jacobson's organ** in their mouth. This organ "tastes" chemicals in the air, especially those produced by other goats in the breeding season. Their sense of taste is good, too. That allows goats to avoid eating moldy or poisonous food.

Fainting Goats

Fainting goats have a disorder. When young goats of the breed are frightened they become stiff and fall over. The disorder is passed down from the parent goats to their young. Older goats learn to stop falling over by spreading their legs or by leaning against something solid, such as a tree trunk.

Fainting goats first came to Marshall County, Tennessee, in the early 1800s. Although raised for their meat, fainting goats were also used to protect other—more valuable—animals, such as sheep. When a predator is on the prowl, the fainting goats get scared and fall over. They are then attacked by the predator, which allows the sheep to escape. Every year in October, fainting goats are honored with a Fainting Goat Festival in Marshall County.

Fainting goats have many other names, including Tennessee meat goats, nervous goats, and wooden-leg goats.

Goats make excellent and affectionate pets.

Nanny and Nanko

Companion breeds of goats make ideal pets. These include pygmy, Nigerian dwarf, and Australian miniature goats. These breeds are much smaller than the dairy and meat breeds.

In the 1860s, Tad and Willie, the sons of Abraham Lincoln, kept goats as pets inside the White House. Two goats called Nanny and Nanko had been given to the Lincoln family. Tad and Willie used to hitch the goats to carts or kitchen chairs and drive them through the White House. They caused a lot of commotion at White House receptions. President Lincoln liked to play with the boys and their goats. While good pets, the goats could also be naughty. Nanko got into trouble by digging up the bulbs in the garden. One day Nanny went missing and was never found. President Lincoln wrote to his wife, who was away. He expressed to her his sadness that the goat had disappeared.

Anything Eaten!

Most people think that goats will eat anything including laundry and garbage! In fact, they are quite picky about what they eat. Goats have a **prehensile** upper lip and tongue. That means that they can grasp things with their upper lip and tongue. They will nibble at most things, including clothes, before deciding whether to eat them or not. Goats prefer to graze on grass or browse on the young leaves and branch tips of trees and shrubs. These animals have a digestive system that can break down, or digest, almost any kind of plant material, including wood. Goats can even eat plants that are poisonous to other animals. For this reason, goats are often used to clear weeds and undergrowth from areas of land.

On some farms, goats are kept indoors. These goats are very particular eaters. They will not eat food that is dirty or has been trampled on. They prefer the best quality hay or a mix of oats, barley, and linseed. This kind of feed is very expensive, which is why most goat farmers prefer their goats to range freely outdoors!

Chewing the Cud

Goats have a four-chambered stomach. That allows them to digest their food in several stages. Many other animals have this kind of stomach, too, including cows, sheep, bison, giraffes, deer, and antelope. These animals do not really chew their food when they graze or browse. Instead, they swallow it quickly. The food enters the first stomach chamber, called the **rumen**. Not having to chew allows these animals to eat continuously, only stopping if they become alarmed.

Later, usually when the animals are resting, the food in the rumen travels back up into the mouth. There, the soggy ball of food, or **cud**, is chewed properly and swallowed again. It then passes through the other chambers of the stomach, where it is broken down further. Bacteria in the stomach produce substances that break down tough, fibrous plant matter. Without these bacteria, the animal would not be able to extract as many nutrients from its food.

A nanny goat is very protective of her kid.

Kids' Food

A kid feeds on milk produced by its mother. The baby goat's digestive system is very different from an adult goat's. That's because digesting milk is different from digesting plant fiber.

When a kid is born, the first chamber of its stomach—the rumen—is small. Milk travels directly through the first three stomach chambers into the fourth chamber. This chamber, called the **abomasum**, is the largest of the kid's stomach chambers. There, milk is digested. When the kid is one or two weeks old, it starts to eat some solid plant food. The rumen then has to grow bigger to cope with all the plant food. By the time the kid becomes an adult, the rumen is the largest of the four stomach chambers.

The first milk that a nanny produces for her kid contains substances that help protect the kid from disease.

A healthy goat should be alert with a clean, well-groomed coat.

Health Check

Goats are usually healthy animals. A healthy goat can live to 14 years old. However, goats do suffer from some common illnesses. It is important for a goat owner or farmer to check on their goats' health every day. A healthy goat is bright eyed, curious about its surroundings, and has a healthy appetite for food and water. An ill goat might smell or sound different from how it does normally. If it is injured, it might have swelling, or limp or walk uncomfortably. In such cases, a vet, or animal doctor, should examine the animal.

Vets routinely give goats **vaccinations** to prevent common infections. They give medicine for any worm infestation, which is a common problem with goats. In addition, vets check goats for insects called lice. These pests cause the goats a lot of irritation and damage to their skin.

Sick Goats

One incurable disease that goats can get is caprine (KAH-PREEN) arthritis encephalitis, or **CAE**. The word *caprine* comes from the Latin word for "goat." *Arthritis* (AHR-THRY-TUS) means "swelling of joints," such as in the legs. And *encephalitis* (IN-SEH-FUH-LIE-TUS) means "swelling of the brain." This nasty disease is caused by a **virus**. The virus spreads between goats when they touch one another. It is also passed onto kids when they nurse from an infected nanny.

In the early stages, CAE is difficult to detect. Infected goats do not have a fever, and they often continue to feed as usual. However, after some time, the goats' muscles begin to waste away. Their leg joints become painful and swollen. The disease may cause nannies to stop producing milk. Once a goat is infected with CAE, it has the disease for life.

Many goats have regular blood tests to check that they have not caught the disease. If a whole herd of goats is infected, they all may have to be slaughtered.

Bottle-feeding a kid can help prevent the spread of CAE.

Hygiene is very important when milking goats. The suction cups that draw milk from the teats of the nannies' udders should be disinfected after each milking.

Nanny Diseases

Nanny goats sometimes suffer from a disease called **mastitis** (MAH-STY-TUS), which stops them from producing milk. All nannies have a special organ called an **udder**, which holds milk. The udder hangs down between, and just in front of, the back legs. Mastitis is usually caused by an infection. It makes the udder swollen and painful. If it is not treated, the infection can spread and eventually kill the nanny. To prevent mastitis, nannies must be milked in a dry, clean area. The hands of anyone milking a goat or the milking-machine attachments need to be very clean, too. If a nanny does become infected, she can be treated with medicines.

Pregnant nannies can suffer from a serious disease called **ketosis** (KEY-TOE-SUS). If a growing kid inside the nanny takes up too much room, it presses on her stomach. The stomach cannot then hold much food. The nanny starts to burn up her own body fat for energy. That produces harmful chemicals that can kill the nanny. To prevent ketosis, pregnant nannies must be well fed.

Breeding Season

Nanny goats are ready to breed, or have their own young, at about one year old. In some places, goats can breed at any time of the year. In the United States, however, the breeding season starts when the day length shortens in fall. When a nanny wants to mate she stays near a billy goat and wags her tail. She calls out a lot and might stop eating her food. She acts like this for three days.

During the breeding season, billy goats enter a period known as the "**rut**." They fight one another, lose their appetite, and become very interested in the nannies. They also develop an unpleasantly strong odor, which they use to mark their territory. If billies are kept with nannies, the males' strong scent can taint, or affect the taste of, the nannies' milk.

Two young African pygmy billies play-fight. When they are older, their fights will be over territory and nannies.

When a nanny goat is pregnant, she is said to be "settled."

Pregnancy

A nanny goat is pregnant for about 150 days. The first time she delivers, a young nanny will give birth to one or two kids. Older nannies tend to have twins or occasionally triplets. Very rarely, they have quadruplets. As well as age, the number of kids depends on how well fed the nanny is. Some farmers control the amount of food that their nannies eat, so that they produce just one kid.

During pregnancy, kids are carried inside a fluid-filled sac inside the nanny. This sac protects them as they grow and develop. All goats, especially pregnant nannies, should be treated gently because goats can become stressed very easily. Some goat owners even sing to their goats to keep them calm. A calm nanny is more likely to stay healthy and have healthy kids.

Only Kidding

Just before giving birth a nanny will breathe heavily, seem worried, and become restless. When she about to give birth, she lies down. Inside her, the fluid-filled sac surrounding the kid breaks. Soon after, the kid is born. Kids are usually born with their head tucked between their front legs. If they are in a different position, they may not be able to come out, and the nanny will need help.

Once the kid is born, the nanny cleans the kid by licking it. That encourages the kid to breathe, and helps it to create a bond with its mother. The nanny soon begins to produce milk. The kid instinctively knows where to find its mother's milk and how to suckle.

By the age of 10 to 12 weeks, kids are fully **weaned**. That means their diet of milk has now been completely replaced by the same plant diet of the adult goats.

Leaping for joy—like most young mammals kids have a lot of energy and love to play.

A goat's horns are hollow. In the past, people used them as containers for liquids and gunpowder.

Horns and Hooves

Most kids are born with small buds on their head that soon start to grow into horns. Many goat owners have their goats' horns removed. That prevents the kids from hurting other goats or humans—horns can be pretty dangerous weapons. The horns are removed with a hot iron. It is usually done to kids when they are between two and seven days old. Once burned, the kids' horns will never grow. Goats with horns tend to bully goats that have had their horns removed, so they should be kept apart.

A goat's hooves grow continuously. This constant growth is very good for wild goats, which wear them down by scrambling over rough ground. However, most domestic goats do not travel around so much. Therefore, they do not wear down their hooves. The hooves of domestic goats need to be trimmed several times a year. Otherwise, they get so long that the goats cannot walk or run properly.

Home for a Goat

Domestic goats need a wind-free shelter that will protect them from the sun, rain, and snow. Each goat needs at least 15 square feet (4.5 sq m) of floor space inside the shelter. Miniature goats need 10 square feet (3 sq m). All domestic goats should have an exercise yard that is four to five times the area of the shelter. They must always have water to drink, too.

Goats can jump up to 5 feet (1.5 m) high. They are good climbers, too. They will nibble at everything. It is important to make a shelter and anywhere a goat has access to nibble-proof. Metal fittings should be used to secure gates and doors because a goat can easily chew through a rope. To keep kids amused, a small bench or table that they can jump onto or lie underneath should be provided. Goats are herd animals and like to have companions, so it is best to keep more than one goat.

A goat shelter can be a simple construction, such as this one built for a Caradoc billy.

This dairy goat has been awarded a ribbon at a farm show.

Show Goats

Shows are the places where breeders can show off their best goats. The goats are judged on certain characteristics. Some of these are body shape, milk productivity, udder quality, muscle quality, and hair quality. The goats with the best qualities for their breed are awarded trophies.

The American Dairy Goat Association (ADGA) uses "Dairy Goat Scorecards" to judge goats. Goats can score up to 100 points on a range of characteristics. Other associations have different scorecards for different types of goats. The kids of award-winning parents usually sell for a lot of money.

Sometimes, there are goat shows for children. Children's shows often have a showmanship class. The goats and their handlers are judged on how well the goats are presented and how well they are handled. The breed of each goat is not important at a children's show.

Legendary Goats

Goats are featured in many myths and legends. One of the Greek gods, Pan, had the legs and horns of a goat. Zeus, the king of the Greek gods, was nursed with the milk of a nanny goat called Amalthea. When Amalthea died, Zeus used her skin to make his thunder-shield. Her horn became the "horn of plenty," overflowing with fruit and grain. Amalthea rose to the heavens to become the constellation Capricorn, which is also the tenth sign of the zodiac.

However, goats didn't always have such a dazzling reputation. In the Middle Ages in Europe, the devil was often shown as a goat!

Whether from myths and legends or raised as farm animals, for shows, or as pets, goats are among the best-known and best-liked animals in the world today. Without doubt, these useful animals will continue to be so for many years to come.

Words to Know

Abomasum The fourth chamber of a goat's stomach.

Bacteria Microscopic single-celled life-forms.

Billies Male goats.

Breeds Particular kinds of goats, each kind with its own characteristics.

CAE Caprine arthritis encephalitis—an incurable disease of goats.

Cashmere A breed of goat from the Himalayas with a soft undercoat of hair; the name of the soft hair.

Cud Swallowed food that is brought back into the mouth for further chewing.

Digest To break down food to get nutrients.

Domesticated Tamed and bred by humans.

Jacobson's organ An area in a goat's mouth that allows it to "taste" chemicals in the air.

Ketosis A disease in which a pregnant goat's body burns up its own fat.

Kids Baby goats.

Lactose A sugar found in milk.

Mastitis A disease in which a nanny goat's udder is swollen and painful.

Mate To come together to produce young.

Nannies Female goats.

Neutered Given a procedure to stop an animal from being able to produce young.

Pasteurized When milk is heated to kill germs.

Prehensile Able to grasp or grip things.

Rumen The first chamber of a goat's four-chambered stomach.

Rut The time of the year when male animals become excited and fight one another over females.

Territorial Describing an animal that defends its own private space.

Udder The part of a goat that holds its milk.

Vaccinations Substances given to animals that protect them against diseases.

Weaned When a young animal no longer drinks its mother's milk.

Find Out More

Books

Miller, S. S. *Goats*. True Books: Animals. Danbury, Connecticut: Children's Press, 2001.

Stone, T. *Goats*. Wild Wild World. San Diego, California: Blackbirch Press, 2003.

Web sites

Goat
www.enchantedlearning.com/subjects/mammals/goat/Goatprintout.shtml
Facts about goats and a diagram to print.

Mammals: Goat and Sheep
www.sandiegozoo.org/animalbytes/t-goat_sheep.html
Information about goats and their relatives, sheep.

Index